LIFE AND LEG.

OF

ROBIN WILLIAMS

JAMIE E.SANDERS

TABLE OF CONTENTS

INTRODUCTION

If you are a fan of the famous actor
and comedian Robin Williams,then this amazing
biography book is for you.

This book will make you understand the many facts
of Robin Williams' contribution to the entertainment
industry in the United States of America.

Robin Williams was famous and cherished ,
known for his unmatched comedic ability,
improvisational abilities, and flexible acting skills.
Brought into the world on July 21, 1951, in Chicago,
Illinois, Williams was brought up in a family with a
solid creative foundation, which without a doubt
impacted his initial interest in performing
expressions.

Williams' profession in diversion started with
stand-up comedy during the 1970s, where he
immediately earned respect for his fire
conveyance, novel voices, and capacity to
consistently progress between various characters
and personas.

He prompted various appearances on TV
programs and in the end a leading edge job as the
outsider Mork in the hit sitcom "Mork and Mindy,"
which launched him to fame.

While Williams at first acquired notoriety as a comic, he exhibited his striking acting reach with jobs in both comedic and sensational movies.

He got basic praise for his exhibitions in motion pictures, for example, "Good Morning, Vietnam," "Dead Poets Society," "The Fisher King" and "GoodWill Hunting," for which he won an Academy Award for Best Supporting Actor.

Williams' capacity to consistently switch a comedy and dramatization exhibited his outstanding ability and profundity as an entertainer.

Notwithstanding his outcome in film and TV, Williams had a huge effect on the universe of liveliness. He gave the voice to the notable Genie in Disney's "Aladdin," a job that permitted him to feature his improvisational abilities and comedic virtuoso.
The person became perhaps Williams' most critical and dearest job, having an enduring impact on crowds, all things considered.

Past his work in amusement, Williams was additionally known for his generosity and devotion to worthy missions. He upheld different associations zeroed in on compassionate endeavors, kids' wellbeing, and natural protection.

Robin's liberality and obligation to having a beneficial outcome on the world further charmed him to fans and partners alike.

Unfortunately, Robin Williams died on August 11, 2014, abandoning a legacy that proceeds to rouse and engage crowds around the world.

His inauspicious passing started an incredible overflow of pain from fans, companions, and individual performers, featuring the significant effect he had on the existence of .

Williams' effect on media outlets is vast, and his commitments keep on being commended through his ageless exhibitions.
His capacity to give pleasure and giggling to individuals' lives, combined with his certified warmth and empathy, cemented his status as a darling figure whose legacy will persevere for a long time into the future.

Robin Williams will continuously be recognized as a genuine legend whose ability, humor, and graciousness contacted the hearts of millions all over the planet.

Chapter One

Early Life And Childhood

Robin McLaurin Williams was brought into the world on July 21, 1951, in Chicago, Illinois, to Robert Fitzgerald Williams, a senior leader at Portage Engine Organization, and Laurie McLaurin, a previous model.

He was Anselm J. McLaurin, the governor of Mississippi and senator,'s great-great-grandson. Williams had two stepbrothers, Todd and McLaurin.

Williams spent his youth in a wealthy area in Bloomfield Slopes, Michigan, where he went to Detroit Country Day School. He showed a natural talent for performing and making people laugh from a young age.

Williams' mom depicted him as an "exceptionally cordial kid who was very modest until you got to know him." This confusing nature would turn into a sign of Williams' comedic style in the years to come.

Sadly, Williams' pure adolescence was damaged by the battles of his folks' marriage. While his mother's health problems caused periods of emotional instability, his father's demanding job frequently kept him away from home.

This wild climate negatively affected Williams, and he looked for comfort in parody and going about for the purpose of adapting to his family's difficulties.

In 1963, when Williams was only 12 years of age, his family moved to Tiburon, California, where he went to Redwood Secondary School. Williams first seriously pursued his comedic abilities during his time in high school.

He succeeded in the two scholastics and extracurricular exercises, partaking in the school's theatrics program and in any event, filling in as class president.

Williams went to Claremont McKenna College in Claremont, California, after graduating from high school, where he planned to major in political science.
In any case, his energy for acting and satire before long drove him to move to the School of Marin in Kentfield, California, where he concentrated on theater and leveled up his improvisational abilities under the direction of educator John Houseman.

Williams' initial encounters at the School of Marin would demonstrate instrumental in molding his future profession. He made the friendship that would last a lifetime with fellow aspiring actor and comedian Christopher Reeve there.

The two would later go to the Juilliard School in New York City together, where they concentrated on under prestigious acting mentor John Houseman.

Regardless of his regular ability and energy for performing, Williams battled with self-uncertainty and frailty during his early stages. His apprehension about disappointment and wanting to satisfy others' hopes weighed intensely on him, driving him to look for approval through his comedic attempts.
This internal conflict would turn into a repetitive topic in Williams' life and work, impacting the two his comedic style and emotional exhibitions.

The early loss of his dad during his last year at Juilliard further intensified Williams' close to home battles. The unexpected demise of his dad left him wrestling with significant sadness and a feeling of deserting.

In the years that followed, Williams directed these mind boggling feelings into his specialty, involving humor as a survival technique while likewise diving into hazier, more contemplative material in his emotional jobs.

Notwithstanding the individual difficulties he confronted, Williams' irrefutable ability and attractive stage presence before long grabbed the eye of crowds and industry experts alike.

His early experiences in improv theater and stand-up comedy clubs prepared him for a rapid rise in the entertainment industry.

Williams had made a name for himself as a dynamic and adaptable performer by the middle of the 1970s. He was praised for his distinctive blend of wacky humor and heartfelt insight.

Williams became a household name in 1978, thanks to his breakthrough role as Mork, an eccentric alien from the planet Ork, on the successful television series "Mork & Mindy."

The show's prosperity exhibited Williams' comedic ability as well as set his status as a dearest commonly recognized name. His likable performance as Mork earned him worldwide acclaim and established him as a comedic pioneer.

The experiences Williams had as a child had a significant impact on the multifaceted persona that would come to define his illustrious career. His capacity to imbue giggling with feeling, to track down light in the obscurity, and to interface with crowds on a profoundly human level were completely established in the early stages of his life.

Despite the difficulties he faced, Williams became an iconic figure whose influence extended beyond the entertainment industry. He left behind an imprint that continues to inspire and motivate audiences worldwide.

Family Background And Upbringing

Robin Williams was naturally introduced to a family with a blend of honor and difficulties. His dad, Robert Fitzgerald Williams, was a senior chief at Portage Engine Organization, which gave the family monetary strength and an agreeable way of life.

Nonetheless, his dad's requesting position frequently got him far from home, prompting a feeling of profound distance inside the family.

Williams' mom, Laurie McLaurin, had experience with displaying and carried a feeling of creative energy to the family.

Sadly, she likewise battled with medical problems that prompted times of profound flimsiness, establishing a turbulent climate for Williams and his two relatives, Todd and McLaurin

The family's transition to Tiburon, California when Williams was 12 denoted a huge progress in his young life.

The family's problems persisted despite the idyllic surroundings. This time of disturbance and personal difficulties significantly affected Williams, who looked for shelter in parody and going about for the purpose of adapting to his family's issues.

The confusing idea of Williams' childhood, a blend of honor and personal strife, assumed a crucial part in forming his comedic style and emotional exhibitions.

He gained a profound understanding of joy and pain as a result, which he would later channel into his work, resulting in a distinctive blend of humor and emotion that audiences appreciated.

Williams' childhood additionally affected his own battles with self-uncertainty and weakness. The apprehension about disappointment and the longing to satisfy others' hopes weighed intensely on him, prompting a deep rooted mission for approval through his comedic tries and emotional jobs.

Notwithstanding the difficulties he confronted, Williams' family foundation and childhood furnished him with a rich embroidery of encounters that powered his imagination and illuminated his creativity. It established the groundwork for the multi-layered persona that would characterize his career as an entertainer who could consistently progress from boisterous satire to powerful show, interfacing with crowds on a profoundly human level.

Education And Early interest

On July 21, 1951, Robin Williams was born in Chicago, Illinois.

He went to state supported schools in Lake Woodland, Illinois, preceding moving to Detroit, Michigan, where he went to Detroit Country Day School. Williams then transferred between Claremont McKenna College in California and the Juilliard School in New York City.

Williams went to Juilliard to study theater and worked with renowned acting coach John Houseman.

He became well-known right away for his comedic and improvisational skills. While at Juilliard, Williams lives with individual performer Christopher Reeve, outlining a dependable friendship.

Williams' interest shifted and changed. He enjoyed playing tennis and golf and was an energetic cyclist.

He was in like manner a vivacious finder of contemporary craftsmanship and asserted works by experts like Shepard Fairey and Banksy.

Williams was a fervent ally of admirable missions notwithstanding his energy for artistic expression. He maintained different establishments and causes generally throughout his life, including St. Jude

Children's Research Hospital and the Christopher and Dana Reeve Establishment.

As a rule, Robin Williams was a diverse person with many interests and capacities, including sports and craftsmanship as well as acting and comedy.
His energy everlastingly and commitment to his specialty made him a loved figure in news sources to say the least.

His lightning-quick wit, infectious enthusiasm, and unparalleled capacity for improvisation made him famous.

His comedic genius transmitted through in famous positions, for instance, the speedy talking radio DJ in "Good Morning, Vietnam," the silly genie in Disney's "Aladdin," and the revered Mrs. Doubtfire. Williams' performances frequently combined humanity, compassion, and humor, gaining him worldwide acclaim.

Past his comedic gifts, Williams also showed his shocking acting chops in films like "Dead Poets Society," Good Will Hunting," and "Awakening."

He was striking in his capacity to flawlessly switch among parody and show, and his flexibility and profound profundity captivated competitors.

Williams was well-known for his consideration, generosity, and empathy off-screen. He frequently made visits to hospitals for children in the spirit of his well-known character Patch Adams to jolt and cheer young patients.

Williams' liberal undertakings loosened up to various causes, including biological assurance, veterans' opportunities, and close to home prosperity care.

Notwithstanding his fights with propensity and close to home wellbeing issues, Robin Williams remained a reassuring sign and inspiration for some.

Through his immortal exhibitions, beneficial works, and impact on numerous lives, his legacy continues to live on. Robin Williams will always be remembered as a genuine entertainment legend and a beacon of hope in a world that sometimes seems to be in darkness.

Influence And inspiration

Robin Williams was influenced and inspired by a considerable number of sources generally through his life and calling. His mother, Laurie Williams, who was a former model and entertainer, was one of his first influences.
She enabled his inventiveness and excitement for performing from the beginning, supporting his capacities and developing his love for spoof.

Williams furthermore drew inspiration from astonishing comics, for instance, Jonathan Winters, Richard Pryor, and Lenny Bruce.
He valued their intense method for managing humor, limit pushing style, and ability to permeate parody with social examination.
Williams frequently cited these comedians as models for his own comedic voice and sources of inspiration.

Williams was likewise affected by entertainers like Dustin Hoffman, Charlie Chaplin, and Peter Wenders, notwithstanding joke artists.
He valued their adaptability, dedication to their field, and capacity to effectively portray a large number of characters. Williams attempted to emulate their pivotal displays and obligation to their specialty.

Williams went beyond the world of entertainment to find inspiration in writing, music, and art. He was a given peruser and drew inspiration from makers like Kurt Vonnegut, J.R.R. Tolkien, and Shakespeare. Williams added layers of intricacy to his exhibitions by regularly integrating artistic references and philosophical experiences into his satire and acting.

Williams, an accomplished artist and improvising performer, also found inspiration in music.
He involved music in his work for the purpose of articulation and close to home association, drawing imaginative motivation from jazz, rock, and old style music.

Robin Williams' influences and inspirations were unique and wide, wrapping numerous inventive disciplines and imaginative voices. He is a genuinely unique ability in media outlets since he can join these impacts into his own particular comedic style and acting exhibitions. Williams's legacy continues to inspire hopeful performers and experts to this day, reminding us of the power of creativity, enthusiasm, and the pursuit of imaginative greatness.

Robin Williams' comedic style and approach to acting were also influenced by his personal struggles and encounters. He acquired a significant comprehension of human weakness and endured his fights with dependence and psychological well-being issues, which he diverted much of the time into his exhibitions. Williams' ability to embed humor with feeling and near and dear significance was his own personal impression of inner turmoil and strength.

Another significant influence was Williams' time spent studying at the Juilliard School in New York City, where he honed his craft and developed his improvisational skills. Williams' approach to satire and acting was shaped by his thorough preparation at Juilliard, which gave him a sense of discipline and dedication to his craft. He was also open to a variety of execution styles.

Williams' own experiences as a father and his love for children also had an impact on his comedic sensibilities.
He frequently incorporated childlike wonder and playfulness into his performances because he was inspired by them. Williams' ability to connect with audiences of all ages through his warmth and humor was evidence of his genuine love for people and desire to bring joy and laughter to others.

Williams' selection of jobs and work's topics were additionally impacted by his energy for civil rights and promotion.
He included his establishment as a celebrity to expose issues about huge issues like vagrancy, mental prosperity, and the environment, including comedy as a gadget for social change and

empathy. Williams' commitment to making the world a prevalent spot through his specialty and activism continues to stir others to include their gifts for everybody's advantage.

In conclusion, Robin Williams' arguments were intricate and deeply personal, drawing on a variety of sources, including personal encounters, training, social activism, family, and individual entertainers.
He turned into a cherished and notable figure in media outlets because of his capacity to join these impacts into a solitary comedic voice and acting style. He likewise abandoned a tradition of inventiveness, sympathy, and laughter.

Chapter Two

Rise To Stardom

1. Network Ascension:
With unparalleled talent and charisma, Robin Williams blazed across the entertainment industry. His meteoric rise to stardom was nothing short of meteoric.

2. Luminous Pioneer:
With his innovative performances and enthralling presence, Williams carved a brilliant path through Hollywood, shattering boundaries and redefining comedy.

3. Heavenly Advancement:
From humble starting points to worldwide recognition, Williams' excursion to fame was a heavenly development set apart by valiant innovativeness and unflinching enthusiasm.

4. Celestial Brilliance:
The splendor of Robin Williams focused like a heavenly light, charming crowds all over the planet and hardening his place as a genuine star.

5. Radiant Phenomenon :
Williams' rising to famc was a brilliant peculiarity, energized by his vast energy, fast mind, and

unmatched capacity to interface with crowds on a significant level.

6. Amazing Development:
With a stunning rise onto the diversion scene, Robin Williams immediately turned into an easily recognized name, charming fans with his unequaled ability and irresistible soul.

7. Dazzling Emergency:
Like a cosmic explosion overhead, Williams' prosperity detonated onto the scene, leaving an enduring effect on the universe of satire and acting that keeps on sparkling brilliantly.

8. Cosmic Victory:
Williams' ascent to fame was a vast victory, powered by his remarkable ability, persevering hard working attitude , and unwavering devotion to his art.

9. Sparkling Starburst:
Robin Williams' excursion to fame was a shining starburst of imagination and brightness, enlightening the hearts and brains of crowds all over.

10. Galactic icon:
The meteoric rise to fame of Robin Williams, a galactic icon of comedy and acting, is still evidence of his lasting legacy and timeless appeal.

11. Celestial Lighthouse:

The path that Robin Williams took in his career was like that of a celestial luminary. He made a name for himself in the entertainment industry and made a lasting impression on everyone who saw his work.

12. Heavenly Peculiarity:

Williams' climb to fame was a heavenly peculiarity, described by his unrivaled ability, irresistible humor, and capacity to contact the hearts of crowds around the world.

13. Undefined Genius:

Williams' virtuoso in parody and acting resembled a cloud, continually developing and growing to make new worlds of chuckling and feeling for fans to investigate.

14. Astral Maestro:

Robin Williams was an astral maestro in the realm of diversion, directing exhibitions with such expertise and energy that they appeared to rise above the limits of existence.

15. Luminous Universe:

Williams' star power was genuinely grandiose in nature, emanating outwards to enamor crowds and rouse an age of entertainers to try the impossible.

16. Extraordinary Fame:

Williams' excursion to fame appeared to be practically powerful in its speed and effect, as he immediately turned into a commonly recognized name and darling figure in the diversion world.

17. Icon of the Interstellar Universe: Robin Williams left a lasting legacy that continues to inspire and entertain as an interstellar comedy and acting icon whose influence extended far beyond Earth.

18. Cosmic Pioneer:
Williams pioneered a path through the universe of diversion, pushing limits and testing standards with his inventive exhibitions and unequaled comedic timing.

19. Wonder In The Sky:
Robin Williams was a heavenly marvel, stunning crowds with his speedy mind, irresistible enthusiasm, and capacity to possess characters with profundity and legitimacy.

20. Legacy Of Starlight:
With his timeless performances and long-lasting influence on the entertainment industry, Williams' legacy shines brightly like a starry sky, illuminating the hearts and minds of both old and new fans.

Early Career And Breakthrough Roles

Robin Williams' early career was set apart by his champion exhibitions in different comedic and emotional jobs that displayed his ability and flexibility. A portion of his leading edge jobs include:

1. Mork from Ork -
Williams earned far and wide respect for his job as Mork, an outsider from the planet Ork, in the TV series "Mork and Mindy" (1978-1982). He won the Golden Globe Award for Best Actor in a Musical or Comedy Television Series for his quirky and likable role.

2. " Good Morning Vietnam" (1987) - Williams got basic recognition for his job as Adrian Cronauer, a radio DJ who carries humor and levity to the wireless transmissions during the Vietnam War. The film displayed Williams' improvisational abilities and comedic virtuoso, acquiring him his first Academy Award Nomination For Best Actor.

3. " Dead Poets Society" (1989) -
In this notorious film, Williams played John Keating, a persuasive English educator at an all-young men private academy who urges his understudies to make the most of every opportunity and seek after their interests. Williams' presentation was both

impactful and strong, procuring him another Academy Award Nomination For Best Actor.

4. " The Fisher King' (1991) - Williams conveyed a nuanced and sincerely resounding execution in this show coordinated by Terry Gilliam. He depicted Repel, a vagrant who frames an improbable bond with a radio shock muscle head played by Jeff Scaffolds. Williams' depiction displayed his sensational reach and acquired him basic praise.

Robin Williams became a versatile actor who could seamlessly switch between comedy and drama in these earlier roles.
His unique approach to character portrayal, talent, and charisma all contributed to his continued success in the entertainment industry.

Notable Performance And Characters

Robin Williams was a prolific actor who was known for his exceptional range and adaptability when it came to playing a wide range of characters in various genres.

All through his career, he conveyed various champion exhibitions that displayed his ability, appeal, and comedic virtuoso.

Here are a few remarkable exhibitions and characters that characterized Robin Williams' famous lifetime:

1. "Mork & Mindy" by Mork, from 1978 to 1982:

Williams rose to acclaim with his job as Mork, an erratic and adorable outsider from the planet Ork, in the hit TV series "Mork and Mindy." His depiction of the particular person, known for his expression "Nanu," caught crowds' hearts and displayed Williams' immaculate comedic timing and improvisational abilities.

2. Adrian Cronauer - "Good Morning, Vietnam" (1987):

In this notorious film, Williams played Adrian Cronauer, a radio DJ relegated to engage American soldiers during the Vietnam War. Williams' presentation as the contemptuous and clever DJ carried humor and humankind to a dull and testing period ever. His improvisational style and irresistible enthusiasm acquired him basic praise and his most memorable Foundation Grant designation.

3. John Keating - "Dead Poets Society" (1989): In this transitioning show, Williams depicted John Keating, a motivational English educator at a moderate all-young men private academy.
Keating's strange showing strategies and accentuation on independence and innovativeness profoundly influence his understudies, empowering them to seek after their fantasies.
Williams' presentation as the magnetic and energetic instructor resounded with crowds and acquired him another Foundation Grant selection.

4. Sean Maguire - "GoodWill Hunting" (1997):
Williams portrayed Sean Maguire, a therapist who helps troubled young genius Good Will Hunting, played by Matt Damon, confront his past and find life direction, in this critically acclaimed drama. Williams' depiction of the humane and astute advisor exhibited his sensational profundity and profound weakness. His presentation in the film procured his first Academy Award Nomination for Best Actor.

5. Genie - "Aladdin" (1992):

Williams loaned his voice to the notorious person of Genie in Disney's energized film "Aladdin." His improvisational abilities and comedic energy carried the awesome person to striking life, making Genie one of the most vital and dearest vivified characters ever.

6.Patch Adams - "Patch Adams" (1998):
In this personal satire show, Williams depicted Patch Adams, a genuine specialist who utilizes humor and sympathy to treat patients. Williams' presentation caught the substance of Adams' eccentric way to deal with medication, mixing humor with ardent snapshots of association and compassion.

7. Mrs. Doubtfire - "Mrs. Doubtfire" (1993):
In this dearest comedy film, Williams depicted Daniel Hillard, a striving entertainer who camouflages himself as an English babysitter named Mrs. Doubtfire to invest energy with his youngsters after a separation. Williams ' double exhibition as both Daniel and Mrs. Doubtfire displayed his comedic ability and capacity to carry warmth and humor to complex relational peculiarities.

8. Dr. Malcolm Sayer - "Awakening" (1990):
Williams played Dr. Malcolm Sayer, a neurologist who discovers a drug that temporarily awakens catatonic patients in this powerful drama based on a true story. Williams' depiction of the caring and

devoted specialist exploring moral quandaries and shaping profound associations with his patients featured his flexibility as an emotional entertainer.

9. Armand Goldman - "The Birdcage" (1996):
In this comedy film, Williams featured as Armand Goldman, the proprietor of a drag club in South Oceanside, Miami. Williams' depiction of the showy and cherishing father exploring what is happening when his child declares his commitment to the little girl of a moderate lawmaker displayed his comedic timing and capacity to track down humor in testing conditions.

10. Teddy Roosevelt - "Night at the museum "series (2006-2014):
In this family-accommodating experience films, Williams gave the voice to the wax figure of President Theodore Roosevelt that shows signs of life around evening time in a gallery. His appealing and exuberant depiction of the notorious authentic figure added humor and appeal to the fantastical reason of the films.

11. Parry- "The Fisher King"(1991): In this dream show coordinated by Terry Gilliam, Williams played Parry, a vagrant experiencing daydreams after a horrible mishap. Williams received critical acclaim for his nuanced performance as the eccentric and vulnerable Parry, which explored themes of redemption and connection. It also demonstrated

his ability to tackle roles that are both complex and emotionally resonant.

12. Alan Parrison - "Jumanji" (1995): In this dream experience film, Williams featured as Alan Parrish, a man caught in a mystical tabletop game for quite a long time who is delivered into this present reality by two youngsters who accidentally release confusion. Williams' depiction of the clever and bold Alan exploring the risks of the game featured his capacity to offset humor with snapshots of veritable inclination and chivalry.

These are only a couple of instances of the numerous essential exhibitions and characters that Robin Williams rejuvenated all through his vocation. He was a beloved and respected actor whose legacy continues to inspire audiences all over the world. His unrivaled improvisational skills, his profound emotional depth, and his seamless transition between comedy and drama made him a beloved and respected actor.

Robin Williams' assorted and critical exhibitions across film, TV, and movement have made a permanent imprint on mainstream society and keep on being commended by crowds, all things considered. His legacy as a talented entertainer,comedian, and narrator perseveres through the immortal characters he rejuvenated on screen.

Impact on the entertainment industry

Robin Williams significantly affected media outlets, passing on an enduring inheritance that proceeds to rouse and impact ages of entertainers, comedians,and storyteller.Here are a few parts of his effect:

1. Versatility:
Robin Williams was referred to for his extraordinary adaptability as an entertainer, flawlessly progressing between comedic jobs, sensational exhibitions, and voice acting in enlivened films. His capacity to exemplify a great many characters with profundity and realness displayed his enormous ability and made him a sought-after ability in Hollywood.

2. Comedic Genius:
Williams was loved as a comedic genius, known for his quick fire improvisational abilities, clever humor, and irresistible enthusiasm in front of an audience and screen. His stand-up satire schedules were incredible, and his comedic timing and capacity to improvise were unparalleled. Williams' remarkable mix of actual parody, pleasantry, and observational humor put him aside as one of the best joke artists of his time.

3. Famous Characters:

Williams created a wide range of well-known characters throughout his career that are now ingrained in popular culture. From the quick talking Genie in "Aladdin" to the adorable Mrs. Doubtfire in the film of similar name, Williams' characters reverberated with crowds and had an enduring effect.

5. Magnanimity and Promotion:
Past his work in diversion, Robin Williams was additionally known for his altruistic endeavors and support work. He upheld various magnanimous associations zeroed in on issues like vagrancy, psychological wellness mindfulness, and youngsters' medical care. Williams utilized his foundation to bring issues to light and assets for purposes near his heart, showing his obligation to having a constructive outcome past the screen.

6. Inspiration:
Robin Williams propelled incalculable yearning entertainers, humorists, and craftsmen with his ability, hard working attitude, and enthusiasm for narrating. His valor in taking on testing jobs, pushing imaginative limits, and associating with crowds on a profound close to home level filled in as a wellspring of motivation for the overwhelming majority in media outlets.
The industry continues to be inspired by Williams' dedication to his craft and ability to bring joy and laughter to millions of people worldwide.

In general, Robin Williams' effect on media outlets is vast. His heritage as a flexible entertainer, comedic virtuoso, caring backer, and rousing figure will keep on resounding long into the future, helping us to remember the extraordinary force of narrating and the persevering through impact of a really gifted craftsman.

Chapter 3

Personal Life

Robin Williams, brought into the world on July 21, 1951, in Chicago, Illinois, had a rich and complex individual life that influenced his calling and associations.

A few insights into Robin Williams' own life are as follows:

1. Family Ancestry:
Robin McLaurin Williams' parents were former model Laurie McLaurin and Ford Motor Company senior executive Robert Fitzgerald Williams. From his father's previous marriage, he had two more experienced step brothers.

Williams' life as a youngster was separate by honor and extravagance, at this point he regularly felt isolated and struggled with vibes of sadness and vulnerability.

2. Education:

Williams went to state subsidized schools in Lake Woodlands, Illinois, where he succeeded academically and showed an early interest in acting and comedy.

From that point forward, he went to Claremont McKenna School and the School of Marin, and he proceeded to concentrate on the auditorium at the Juilliard School in New York City.

3. Marriages and Children: Throughout his life, Robin Williams was married multiple times. His 1978 marriage to Valerie Velardi, with whom he had a son named Zachary, is his most famous marriage.

In 1988, the couple got separated. Williams then married Marsha Garces in 1989, with whom he had two children, Zelda and Cody. In 2010, they parted ways. In 2011, Williams married Susan Schneider, who remained his soul mate until his death in 2014.

4.Struggles With Addiction And Mental Health:
All through his life, Robin Williams battled with reliance on meds and alcohol, which he as often as possible used as a step by step process for surviving for his hazards and melancholy. In interviews and public appearances, he made it abundantly clear that he was struggling with addiction and had multiple times sought treatment for substance abuse and mental health issues.

5. Charity work

Robin Williams was known for his philanthropic undertakings and sponsorship for various unselfish affiliations. He routinely partook in fund-raising events for purposes like vagrancy, young people's clinical benefits, and profound wellbeing care. Williams used his whiz status to bring issues to light and resources for affiliations like St. Jude Children's Research Hospital and Comic Relief.

6. Recreation Exercises And Interests:

Past his acting calling, Robin Williams had different relaxation exercises and interests that gave him joy and loosening up. He was an excited cyclist, painter, and finder of memorabilia. Williams similarly had an energy for PC games and development, much of the time lowering himself in virtual universes as a kind of takeoff from the pressures of reputation.

7. Effect and legacy:

Robin Williams' sudden downfall by implosion in 2014 paralyzed the world and shed light on the fights he stood up to with sadness and profound prosperity issues. His passing sparked discussions regarding the significance of emotional well-being mindfulness and the destigmatization of dysfunctional behavior-related conversations. Fans and individual craftsmen overall keep on being enlivened by Williams' inheritance as a skilled entertainer, caring backer, and beloved diversion figure.

As a rule, Williams' own life was separated by wins and troubles, wins and setbacks. His straightforwardness about his fights with obsession and mental prosperity, joined with his obligation to his strength and philanthropic endeavors, left a persevering through impact on the people who knew him eventually and individuals who regarded him from a far distance. Williams' legacy as a diverse craftsman, devoted husband, and benevolent friend endures as evidence of his enduring influence on the entertainment industry.

Relationship And Marriages

Robin Williams had three gigantic relationships and connections generally through his life, each expecting a crucial part in significantly shaping his own life and livelihood. The following are individual experiences that shed light on Robin Williams' relationships and connections:

1. Valerie Velardi (1978-1988):
In the 1970s, when Robin Williams was as yet a rising star in media outlets, he met Valerie Velardi. They got hitched in 1978, and their relationship was separated by love, laughing, and shared interests.

- The couple welcomed their most essential youth, Zachary, in 1983. Williams was known to be a serious father and family man, habitually contributing quality energy with his youngster no matter what his mentioning work plan.

- Regardless, their marriage went up against troubles due to Williams' creating praise, busy shooting schedules, and fights with substance abuse. Reports of untrustworthiness on Williams' part furthermore focused on their relationship.

- Ultimately, the couple separated in 1988 following 10 years of marriage. Williams and Velardi continued to be supportive co-guardians of their son, Zachary, despite the breakup of their close friendship.

2. Marsha Garces (1989-2010):

- Following his partition from Valerie Velardi, Robin Williams began a relationship with Marsha Garces, who was filling in as a sitter for his youngster Zachary. Garces later became Williams' partner, and their professional collaboration developed into a sincere relationship.

- Williams and Garces got the pack in 1989, and they continued to have two youths together, Zelda and Cody. The family radiated an impression of being a friendly unit, with Williams embracing his occupation as a father and companion.

- Regardless, their marriage defied challenges all through the long haul, recalling blabber-mouthy goodies about untrustworthiness as far as it matters for Williams and strains achieved by his ceaseless battles with oppression and profound prosperity issues.

- In 2008, following twenty years of marriage, Williams and Garces requested for lawful partition, referring to threatening differences. Despite the end of their sincere kinship, they kept a co-supporting relationship focused on the flourishing of their youths.

3. Susan Schneider: From 2011 to 2014

- In the later significant stretches of his life, Robin Williams found love again with Susan Schneider, a visual fashioner and expert. The couple met through normal mates and quickly related over shared interests and a significant up close and personal bond.

In 2011, Williams and Schneider secured the group at a private event attended by loved ones. Their relationship was depicted by normal respect, companionship, and support during Williams' nonstop fights with melancholy and clinical issues.

- Williams had Schneider close by as he battled with his moderation, emotional wellness, and vocation pressures. She expected a basic part in helping him with investigating irksome times and invigorating up close and personal.

- Unfortunately, Robin Williams' life came to a not great resolution in 2014 when he passed on by implosion. Schneider was devastated and grieving the loss of her closest partner when he passed away.

All things considered, Robin Williams' associations and connections were separated by veneration, chuckling, hardships, and complexities natural in any human affiliation. His assistants accepted basic parts in his everyday presence, offering assistance, understanding, and kinship through the high points and low points of his own and capable outing.

Despite the ups and downs of his romantic relationships, Williams' legacy as a devoted father, committed partner, and talented performer endures as evidence of his profound impact on those closest to him.

Challenges And Struggles

Throughout his life, Robin Williams experienced numerous personal and professional issues that had a significant impact on his relationships, career, and overall health. The following are a couple of basic troubles and individual fights that Williams grappled with:

1. Substance Abuse:
   - Robin Williams' battle with substance abuse may have been one of his most notable battles. He had a long history of reliance on prescriptions and alcohol, which began during his underlying seemingly forever in news sources.
   - Williams' issues with substance misuse as often as possible stressed his associations with his accomplices and family. His fixation likewise affected his work, upsetting his vocation and influencing the two his psychological and actual wellbeing.

2. Mental health issues:
   - Despite substance abuse, Robin Williams struggled with profound health issues generally throughout his life. He talked authentically about his battles with misery and uneasiness, which regularly showed themselves in times of outrageous pity and disturbance.

- Williams' mental health challenges affected his own life as well as influenced his work as a performer and performer. He managed his inward contentions through humor for adapting, yet under the chuckling was a lot of profound aggravation.

3. Problems in relationships:

- Williams' associations were not safe to challenge, as his fame, involved schedule, and individual fights habitually put a weight on his genuine associations. His relationships every now and again highlighted charges of disloyalty, breakdowns in correspondence, and close to home distance.

Williams' connections endured because of the pressure of managing compulsion and emotional wellness issues simultaneously as keeping a fruitful vocation. Despite his significant love for his associates and youths, these hardships added to the breakdown of his connections.

4.Career Pressures:

- As a significantly productive and dearest performer and comedian, Robin Williams defied massive strain to convey extraordinary presentations and stay aware of his status as a comedic image. He was extremely burdened by the demands of popularity, ongoing public scrutiny, and exclusive standards from fans and critics.

- Williams' hair splitting and need to fulfill others every so often incited self-vulnerability and unsteadiness about his gifts. He had trouble with the pressure to always be "on " and make people laugh, even when he was fighting internal demons.

5. Medical problems

- Despite his mental prosperity, Robin Williams also faced different clinical issues all through the long haul. He had a foundation set apart by heart issues, as well as different illnesses that normal treatment and checking.

- Williams' prosperity moves added another layer of unpredictability to his inside and out frustrated life, anticipating that he should balance dealing with oneself with the solicitations of his employment and individual associations.

Despite these hardships and individual fights, Robin Williams continued to give joy, laughing, and inspiration to swarms all around the planet through his comedic virtuoso and ability to act. His ability to find humor despite setbacks and connection point with people on a significant near and dear level excess parts a getting through legacy that transcends the difficulties he thoroughly searched in his own life.

6. Financial Problems:

- No matter what his huge advancement in news sources, Robin Williams went up against money related troubles at better places in his everyday presence. Reports suggested that he encountered money related difficulties as a result of sumptuous spending, bombarded hypotheses, and excessive detachments.

- Williams's financial struggles made his already complicated life more stressful, forcing him to keep working to support his family and maintain his lifestyle. The strain to help his occupation and pay could have added to his overall thriving and close to home prosperity.

7. Depression and Disengagement:

Robin Williams frequently experienced feelings of loneliness and separation, despite the fact that he was surrounded by fans, partners, and friends and family. His comedic persona and astonishing person at times hidden his internal impressions of opening and confinement.

- Williams' fights with disheartening could have been exacerbated by the solicitations of his work, which anticipated that he should travel routinely and burn through broad stretches away from home. The troubles of staying aware of critical affiliations and finding credible companionship added to his significant loads.

8. Self-Vulnerability and insecurities

- Behind the outside of humor and persona, Robin Williams grappled with immovably settled self-vulnerability and insecurities about his capacity and worth. He battled with insecurities and a consistent requirement for approval notwithstanding his gigantic achievement.

- Williams' hair-splitting and drive for greatness were frequently fueled by internal evil spirits, forcing him to constantly seek approval and validation from others. His fights with certainty and sureness could have added to his close to home prosperity issues and individual challenges.

9. Guilt And Regret
- All through his life, Robin Williams conveyed a sensation of culpability and regret about various pieces of his past. Whether associated with his associations, work decisions, or individual choices, he every now and again grappled with vibes of disappointment and self-issue.

The effect Williams' activities had on others, as well as botched open doors or yearnings, may have added to his battles with culpability and lament. These agitated sentiments added another design to his inside and out wild inward world.

10. Heritage and Endlessness:
- As a treasured figure in news sources, Robin Williams stood up to the trial of obliterating his public image with his classified fights. He felt a great deal of strain to carry on a decent inheritance and be associated with his commitments.

Williams's desire for immortality through his work and influence on others may have influenced his choices and actions throughout his life. His close to home excursion and individual battles turned out to be more intricate because of his nervousness about being neglected or misconstrued.

His perseverance as a comedic virtuoso, gifted entertainer, and sympathetic person continues to inspire and resonate with crowds all over the world, despite the numerous challenges and personal struggles he faced. His ability to convey chuckling and light to the world, even in the midst of his own dinkiness, remains a show of his flexibility and overcoming soul.

Chapter 4

Legacy in Comedy

Robin Williams' inheritance in parody is completely unbelievable, as he is broadly viewed as one of the best comedic abilities ever.

He stands out as a true master of his craft because of his distinctive combination of witty humor, boundless energy, and rapid-fire improvisation. Here are a few vital parts of Robin Williams' getting through heritage in the realm of satire:

1. Creative Comedy Style:
   - Robin Williams altered the satire scene with his creative and capricious style. His quick fire conveyance, continuous flow talks, and capacity to flawlessly switch among characters and voices exhibited his unrivaled comedic virtuoso.

   - Williams' improvisational abilities were unparalleled, as he could easily make comical and important minutes on the spot. His capacity to think and react quickly and draw in with crowds in an unconstrained and dynamic way separate him as a comedic pioneer.

2. Famous Comedic Performances:
   - Robin Williams' stand-up parody exhibitions are unbelievable and have made a permanent imprint on the universe of satire. From his initial days acting in parody clubs to sold-out field shows,

Williams charmed crowds with his zapping presence and unequaled ability.

- Exemplary stand-up specials like "Robin Williams: Inhabit the Met" and "Robin Williams: Live on Broadway" feature his comedic brightness and extremely sharp mind. His capacity to handle a great many points with humor and understanding set his standing as a comedic force to be reckoned with.

3. Significant Characters And Impressions:

- All through his profession, Robin Williams made a huge number of essential characters and impressions that have become famous in mainstream society. Williams demonstrated his versatility and talent as a performer in roles like "Mrs. Doubtfire" and "Aladdin," where he played the beloved Mork from the sitcom "Mork & Mindy."

- Williams' capacity to possess different characters and rejuvenate them with humor and heart charmed him to crowds, everything being equal. His reach as an entertainer and comic permitted him to rise above limits and interface with individuals on a profoundly close to home level.

4. Influence on People in the future:

- Robin Williams' impact on people in the future of comics and entertainers is endless. Numerous entertainers refer to him as a significant impact and motivation, lauding his valor, innovativeness, and obligation to his art.

- Williams' eagerness to push limits, tackle delicate subjects, and use humor as an instrument for social discourse made ready for another age of comics to investigate their own special voices and viewpoints. His inheritance keeps on moving hopeful comics right up 'till now.

5. Helpful Endeavors and Generosity:
- Notwithstanding his comedic gifts, Robin Williams was known for his magnanimous endeavors and compassionate work. He utilized his foundation and impact to help different admirable missions, including associations zeroed in on psychological well-being, mindfulness, vagrancy, and kidz' medical services.
- Williams' obligation to reward those out of luck and involving his voice for positive change embodies his caring nature and liberal soul. His inheritance reaches out past the domain of parody, leaving an enduring effect on the existences of those he contacted through his charitable undertakings.

Generally, Robin Williams' legacy in comedy is characterized by his unrivaled ability, pivotal exhibitions, and persevering through influence on the universe of amusement. His capacity to give pleasure, giggling, and sympathy to crowds all over the planet will everlastingly solidify his status as a comedic symbol and dearest figure in mainstream society.

Contributions To Comedy And improvisation

With his unparalleled talent, quick wit, and boundless creativity, Robin Williams redefined comedy and improvisation, which are nothing short of groundbreaking. Here are a few critical parts of his commitments to satire and spontaneous creation:

1. Improvisation Master:
   - Robin Williams was generally viewed as an expert of ad lib, with a remarkable capacity to think and react quickly and make unconstrained, entertaining minutes on the spot. His improvisational abilities were unequaled, permitting him to flawlessly zigzag all around characters, voices, and situations with lightning speed.
   - Williams' improvisational style was a sign of his parody, as he flourished in unscripted conditions and succeeded at drawing in with crowds in a dynamic and erratic way. His fast reasoning and sharp comedic impulses put him aside as a genuine improvisational virtuoso.

2. Continuous flow comedy:
   - One of Robin Williams' mark comedic styles was his continuous flow way to deal with parody, where

he would riff on a great many subjects in a quick fire, non-direct design. His capacity to hop starting with one thought then onto the next with consistent changes kept crowds as eager and anxious as can be and left them to join.

- Williams' continuous flow discourses were a demonstration of his innovative virtuoso and brave way to deal with satire. He would draw motivation from regular daily existence, recent developments, and individual encounters, implanting his exhibitions with suddenness and eccentricism.

3. Character Work and Voices:

- Robin Williams was known for his uncommon ability for making a different cluster of characters and voices in his parody. From kooky self -images to impactful depictions of ordinary individuals, Williams had an uncanny capacity to rejuvenate characters with humor and heart.

- His dominance of voices and accents permitted him to possess a large number of characters, exhibiting his flexibility as an entertainer. Whether playing a vivified genie in "Aladdin" or a dressing-drag babysitter in "Mrs. Doubtfire," Williams' personality work was a demonstration of his comedic reach and acting ability.

4. Joint efforts and Comedy Organizations:

- All through his vocation, Robin Williams worked together with individual entertainers and comedy specialists, making remarkable comedic minutes and exhibitions. His work with comedy bunches like

The Satire Store Players and The Comedy Olympics helped shape his improvisational abilities and cement his standing as a comedic force to be reckoned with.

- Williams' joint efforts with extemporization accomplices like Jonathan Winters, Whoopi Goldberg, and Billy Gem brought about probably the most significant and unconstrained comedic crossroads in amusement history. His capacity to play off others and hoist their exhibitions with his speedy mind and irresistible enthusiasm was a demonstration of his cooperative soul.

5. Tradition of Act of spontaneity:

- Robin Williams' heritage in extemporization keeps on motivating humorists and entertainers all over the planet. His valiant way to deal with parody, obligation to suddenness, and commitment to pushing limits have made a permanent imprint on the craft of act of spontaneity.

Many comedians cite Williams' fearlessness, creativity, and sheer brilliance as guiding lights in their own careers, citing him as a major influence on their own improvisational skills and comedic style. His tradition of act of spontaneity lives on through the incalculable specialists who keep on being enlivened by his noteworthy work.

6. Actual Satire:

- Robin Williams was known for his extraordinary actual parody abilities, integrating overstated developments, looks, and signals into his exhibitions. His capacity to utilize his body as a comedic instrument added an additional layer of diversion to his schedules and exhibited his flexibility as an entertainer.

- Williams' actual parody frequently supplemented his fast fire verbal humor, making a dynamic and drawing in comedic experience for crowds. Whether he was imitating creatures, moving around the stage, or distorting his face into different looks, his rawness added an exceptional aspect to his satire.

7. Comedy as a form of social commentary:

Robin Williams was known for using humor as a vehicle for social commentary and political satire, in addition to his comedic skills. In his stand-up routines, he bravely addressed controversial subjects and current events, shedding light on significant issues while making the audience laugh.

- Williams' capacity to mix humor with powerful perceptions and quick discourse put him unafraid aside as a comic to address testing subjects. His readiness to push limits and challenge cultural standards through parody made him a strong voice in the realm of diversion.

8. Acting improvisationally:

- Past his stir in stand-up parody, Robin Williams additionally exhibited his improvisational abilities in his acting exhibitions. He was known for promoting libbing lines, ad libbing scenes, and getting immediacy to his movies and TV programs.

- Williams' improvisational acting style permitted him to bring a feeling of realness and unusualness to his characters, making them more unique and drawing in for crowds. His capacity to think and react quickly and make do at the time added an additional layer of profundity to his exhibitions.

9. Effect on Comedy Parody Culture:
Beyond his own performances, Robin Williams has had an impact on the world of improv comedy because he helped to shape the culture and community of improv theater. His devotion to the fine art, backing of arising ability, and readiness to face challenges roused another age of improvisers.
- Williams' participation in improv theaters and comedy clubs contributed to the rise of improvisation to the status of a well-respected art form and opened the door for future generations of performers to investigate the plethora of possibilities that can arise from spontaneous creativity. His heritage keeps on affecting the comedy satire scene right up to the present day.

10. Observing Suddenness and Inventiveness:
- Robin Williams' contributions to comedy and improvisation, above all else, celebrate the power of spontaneity, creativity, and performance joy. A lasting legacy that continues to inspire artists and entertain audiences worldwide is left by his fearless approach to comedy, boundless imagination, and infectious energy.

As a reminder of the transformative power of laughter and the significance of embracing spontaneity in creative expression, Williams' capacity to captivate audiences with his quick wit, dynamic characters, and heartfelt performances serves as His inheritance lives on as a demonstration of the persevering through effect of satire and extemporization on the human soul.

All in all, Robin Williams' commitments to satire and acts of spontaneity are a demonstration of his unparalleled ability, imagination, and effect on the universe of diversion. His heritage as a comedic pioneer and improvisational virtuoso will be for all time recalled and celebrated by crowds and craftsmen alike.

Memorable   Comedic Moments And Stand_Up Performances.

Robin Williams was a comedic virtuoso whose critical minutes and stand-up exhibitions have made a permanent imprint on the universe of comedy, Known for his fast fire mind, vast energy, and unrivaled improvisational abilities, Williams' comedic virtuoso radiated through in various critical minutes all through his vocation.

1. Mork and Mindy:

 - One of Robin Williams' breakout jobs was as Mork, an outsider from the planet Ork, in the television series "Mork and Mindy." His depiction of the idiosyncratic and adorable extraterrestrial exhibited his comedic abilities and sent him off into fame. Williams' goofy tricks, wild impromptu creations, and irresistible enthusiasm made the personality of Mork a fan #1 and cemented his standing as a comedic amazing powerhouse.

2. Live at the Met:

 - In 1986, Robin Williams recorded his notable stand-up satire extraordinary "Robin Williams:Live at the Met" at the Metropolitan Drama House in New York City. The exceptional included Williams at the level of his comedic powers, conveying a masterpiece execution that joined quick fire jokes, splendid impressions, and keen social editorial. His capacity to flawlessly change between characters, voices, and points enamored crowds and set his status as a satire legend.

3. Good Morning Vietnam:
   - Williams' job as Pilot Adrian Cronauer in the film "Great Morning, Vietnam" exhibited his special mix of humor and heart. His improvisational abilities were on full showcase as he depicted a plate jockey in war-torn Saigon, infusing humor and humankind into the existences of fighters during the Vietnam War. Williams' exhibition procured him basic praise and a Golden Award for Best Actor in A Motion Picture - Melodic or comedy .

4. Mrs. Doubtfire:
   - In the cherished satire film "Mrs. Doubtfire," Robin Williams assumed the famous part of Daniel Hillard, a separated from father who camouflages himself as a Scottish babysitter to invest energy with his youngsters. Williams' comedic timing, rawness, and capacity to possess numerous characters carried heart and humor to the film. His presentation as Mrs. Doubtfire procured him a Golden Globe Award For Best Actor In A Motion Picture- Melodic or Satire.

5. Aladdin:
   - Robin Williams loaned his voice to the personality of Genie in Disney's enlivened work of art "Aladdin," conveying a significant and comical exhibition that became one of the features of the

film. Williams' improvisational abilities were effectively utilized as he rejuvenated the awesome Genie with mind, enchant, and limitless energy. His presentation as Genie stays a fan number one and a demonstration of his comedic brightness.

6. Comic Relief

- Close by individual jokesters Billy Gem and Whoopi Goldberg, Robin Williams helped to establish the foundation occasion "Lighthearted element," which intended to raise assets for vagrancy mindfulness. Williams' cooperation in the yearly fundraiser displayed his obligation to involve parody for a valuable motivation and featured his liberal soul. His comedic commitments to the Lighthearted element helped raise a great many dollars for those out of luck and cemented his inheritance as a humorist with an endearing personality.

7. The Tonight Show Featuring Johnny Carson:

- Robin Williams showed up on "The This evening Show Featuring Johnny Carson," where he displayed his fast mind, improvisational abilities, and irresistible character. His extemporaneous exhibitions and spur of the moment chit chat with Johnny Carson enchanted crowds and showed his capacity to order the stage effortlessly. Williams' appearances on the show became unbelievable crossroads in late-night TV history and set his standing as a comedic force to be reckoned with.

8. An evening with Robin Williams:

- Throughout his career, Robin Williams participated in a number of lucrative stand-up comedy tours, one of which was "An Evening with Robin Williams." These live exhibitions permitted Williams to associate straightforwardly with crowds, displaying his crude ability, unrestrained energy, and unrivaled comedic ability. His capacity to enamor swarms, his lightning-quick ad libs, clever characters, and sincere narrating made each show a really remarkable encounter.

9. The Casket:

- In the satire film "The Bird enclosure," Robin Williams featured as Armand Goldman, the proprietor of a drag club in South Oceanside, Morning Miami. Williams' depiction of Armand displayed his comedic adaptability and profound profundity, as he explored the intricacies of relational peculiarities and personality with humor and heart. His exhibition in "The Bird enclosure" showed his capacity to carry humankind and humor to even the most difficult circumstances.

10. Stand-Up Comedy

- Robin Williams' heritage as a professional comic is characterized by his brave way to deal with satire, unparalleled improvisational abilities, and relentless obligation to making crowds snicker. His pivotal stand-up schedules keep on motivating humorists all over the planet, setting an exclusive requirement for imagination, creativity, and legitimacy in satire.

Williams' capacity to interface with crowds on a profound close to home level while conveying hilarious humor has solidified his status as one of the best entertainers ever.

Robin Williams' important comedic minutes and stand-up exhibitions will always be esteemed by fans and individual entertainers the same. His heritage as a comedic symbol lives on through his immortal humor, extraordinary characters, and persevering through on the universe of satire.

Influence On Future Generations Of Comedy

Robin Williams was a comedic genius whose effect on people in the future of comedians is significant and persevering. Here are a few critical manners by which Robin Williams has impacted entertainers and formed the comedy scene:

1. Improvisational Abilities:
Robin Williams was known for his unmatched improvisational abilities, fast mind, and capacity to make characters and jokes on the spot. His improvisational style motivated numerous joke artists to embrace suddenness and imagination in their exhibitions.

2. Versatility:
Robin Williams displayed his flexibility as a comic via flawlessly changing between stand-up satire, TV, and film. His capacity to succeed in different comedic designs urged humorists to investigate various stages and types to feature their abilities.

3. Actual Comedy:
Robin Williams was an expert of actual comedy, utilizing his non-verbal communication, looks, and motions to upgrade his exhibitions. His actual satire schedules have roused endless joke artists to integrate rawness into their demonstrations and push the limits of conventional comedy.

4. Profundity and Weakness:

While known for his comedic splendor, Robin Williams likewise showed profundity, weakness, and profound reach in his exhibitions. His capacity to implant humor with crude inclination and legitimacy resounded with crowds and enlivened comics to investigate further subjects in their comedy.

5. Work For Charity:

Past his comedic abilities, Robin Williams was additionally known for his magnanimity and commitment to worthy missions. Many comedians have been inspired to use their platform for social good and make a positive impact on the world by his commitment to giving back to the community and supporting those in need.

In Conclusion, Robin Williams' heritage as a comedic symbol proceeds to rouse and impact ages of jokesters, helping them to remember the force of chuckling, imagination, and empathy in associating with crowds and having an enduring effect on the universe of comedy.

Chapter 5

Acting Career

Robin Williams was a dearest entertainer and humorist known for his staggering ability, flexibility, and energy. He previously rose to notoriety as the outsider Mork in the hit Program "Mork and Mindy" in the last part of the 1970s. His presentation as the kooky, adorable outsider charmed him to crowds and displayed his extraordinary comedic capacities.

Williams' acting profession crossed north of forty years and remembered many jobs for both film and TV. He was known for his capacity to flawlessly progress among satire and show, frequently bringing a special mix of humor and profundity to his characters.

A portion of Williams' most notorious film jobs incorporate his Institute Grant winning execution as specialist Dr. Sean Maguire in "GoodWill Hunting," the unusual Genie in Disney's "Aladdin," the motivational educator John Keating in "Dead Poets Society," and the dressing in drag babysitter Mrs. Doubtfire in the film of a similar name.

Williams' ability was not restricted to the big screen; he likewise had an effective profession in front of an audience, performing stand-up satire and limited shows that displayed his fast mind and improvisational abilities.

All through his vocation, Williams got various honors for his work, including four Brilliant Globe Grants, two Screen Entertainers Organization Grants, and an Institute Grant. His exhibitions were frequently commended for their close to home profundity, realness, and humankind.

Tragically, 63-year-old Robin Williams passed away in 2014. Fans and fellow actors who remembered him as a brilliant performer whose work touched the lives of millions expressed their grief upon hearing of his passing. Williams' heritage keeps on living on through his immortal exhibitions and getting through influence on the universe of diversion.

Robin Williams was known for his humanitarian endeavors and beneficent work. He upheld a large number of causes, including kids' medical clinics, destitute safe houses, and veterans' associations. Williams frequently performed at good cause occasions and pledge drives, involving his comedic gifts to fund-raise and mindfulness for significant causes.

Williams was also an accomplished voice actor who contributed his distinctive voice to animated films like "Happy Feet," "Robots," and "FernGully: The Last Rainforest." His capacity to rejuvenate characters through his voice work added one more aspect to his generally amazing assemblage of work.

Williams' effect on mainstream society was significant, as he impacted an age of entertainers and entertainers with his one of a kind style and way to deal with execution. His capacity to consistently mix humor with genuine inclination reverberated with crowds all over the planet, making him a dearest and getting through figure in media outlets.

Regardless of his battles with sadness and enslavement, Williams stayed devoted to his art and kept on rousing others with his ability and liberality. His heritage fills in as a sign of the force of giggling, sympathy, and imagination in associating individuals and giving pleasure to the world.

Robin Williams will always be remembered as a one-of-a-kind artist whose work continues to inspire, uplift, and entertain audiences of all ages. His commitments to the universe of diversion will be for all time treasured, guaranteeing that his soul lives on through the persevering through effect of his exhibitions.

Iconic Film And Television Performances

Robin Williams was famous for his amazing scope of jobs and unrivaled flexibility as an entertainer. He easily changed between comedic, emotional, and, surprisingly, wretched jobs with equivalent expertise and profundity, displaying his enormous ability and versatility.

In his initial vocation, Williams acquired notoriety for his improvisational comedy abilities and fast fire mind, which he brought to famous jobs like Mork from the TV series "Mork and Mindy." His capacity to think and react quickly and make unconstrained, silly minutes charmed him to crowds and laid him out as a comedic awe-inspiring phenomenon.

As his profession advanced, Williams exhibited his flexibility by taking on a wide assortment of jobs that displayed his emotional abilities to act. He conveyed strong exhibitions in movies, for example, "Good. Morning, Vietnam," "Dead Poets Society," In films like "Mrs. Doubtfire," "Hook," and "Aladdin," where he played the beloved Genie,

Williams' amazing character and unrivaled comedic timing made him a characteristic fit for these endearing and engaging jobs, setting his status as a cherished figure in mainstream society.

Notwithstanding his comedic and emotional work, Williams exhibited his hazier side in movies, for example, "One Hour Photograph" and "A sleeping disorder," where he played chilling and ethically equivocal characters with chilling power. These exhibitions featured his reach as an entertainer and showed his capacity to occupy a wide range of feelings and inspirations on screen.

All through his vocation, Williams ceaselessly pushed the limits of his specialty, bravely handling testing jobs and investigating new sorts and styles. His eagerness to face challenges and trials with various sorts of characters put him aside as a genuinely flexible entertainer who could succeed in any job he embraced.

Robin Williams' scope of jobs and flexibility as an entertainer were really exceptional, solidifying his heritage as perhaps of the best ability throughout the entire existence of film and TV. His capacity to enamor crowds with his humor, heart, and mankind will always be recalled and celebrated by fans all over the planet.

Robin Williams' adaptability as an entertainer reached out past only his on-screen exhibitions. He was likewise a skilled voice entertainer, loaning his particular voice to vivified characters in films like "Aladdin," "Blissful Feet," and "Robots." His capacity to rejuvenate vivified characters with humor, feeling, and profundity further displayed his ability and innovativeness as an entertainer.

Notwithstanding his work in film and TV, Williams likewise left an imprint on the universe of stand-up satire with his charging live exhibitions. His fast fire conveyance, sharp mind, and uncanny capacity to typify a large number of characters and accents made him an unbelievable figure in the satire world. His stand-up specials, like "Live at the Met" and "Weapons of Self-Destruction," made him one of the best comedians ever.

Williams' flexibility was not restricted to acting and satire; he had an enthusiasm for charity and utilized his foundation to advocate for different causes. He upheld associations committed to aiding kids, veterans, and people battling with emotional wellness issues, showing his sympathy and obligation to having a constructive outcome on the world.

Notwithstanding his acting and satire gifts, Williams was likewise a talented improviser, known for his fast reasoning and capacity to make unconstrained, funny minutes on the spot. His improvisational abilities were on full display in films like "Good Morning, Vietnam" and "Mrs. Doubtfire," where he brought a component of immediacy and unusualness to his exhibitions that charmed him to crowds.

Robin Williams' flexibility as an entertainer, humorist, voice craftsman, and giver put him aside as a genuinely diverse ability whose effect keeps on being felt long after his passing. His capacity to succeed in a large number of jobs and classifications, combined with his certifiable warmth and humankind, guaranteed that he would be recognized as a cherished symbol in media outlets for a long time into the future.

Chapter 6

Mental Health Advocacy

Williams was a vocal backer for destigmatizing psychological sickness and empowering people to look for help and backing. He frequently talked openly about his own encounters with discouragement and dependence, sharing experiences into his own fights and the significance of looking for treatment. Williams broke down barriers and sparked discussions about mental health by sharing his story, encouraging others to seek assistance.

As well as bringing issues to light through his public articulations and meetings, Williams likewise upheld different psychological well-being associations and drives. He took part in foundation occasions, pledge drives, and missions pointed toward advancing psychological wellness mindfulness, schooling, and backing administrations. Williams made use of his fame to raise awareness of these pressing issues and inspire others to get involved in the fight against mental illness.

Williams' backing for psychological wellness reached out past his public persona and magnanimous endeavors. Generally speaking, Robin Williams' commitment to emotional wellness promotion left an enduring effect on media outlets and society overall.
Williams' legacy as an emotional well-being advocate keeps on resounding with crowds and stays a significant piece of his influence on the world.

Robin Williams' promotion for psychological well-being was multi-layered and effective, contacting crowds all over the planet through different channels. One striking part of his support was his contribution in bringing issues to light about the significance of looking for help for psychological wellness issues. Williams underlined the meaning of connecting for help, whether through treatment, medicine, or different assets, and urged people to focus on their psychological prosperity.

Notwithstanding his public explanations and good cause work, Williams likewise utilized his comedic gifts to address emotional wellness points in a carefree yet significant manner. Through his stand-up satire schedules and exhibitions, he frequently addressed subjects connected with psychological wellness, offering bits of knowledge and viewpoints that resounded with crowds. By integrating these subjects into his satire, Williams standardized discussions about psychological well-being and made it more available for individuals to examine.

In addition, Williams supported initiatives aimed at enhancing resources and services for mental health. He loaned his voice to crusades elevating admittance to psychological wellness care, diminishing shame, and upholding for strategy changes to more readily uphold people battling with dysfunctional behavior. Williams was able to amplify important messages and effect positive change in the mental health landscape by utilizing his platform and influence.

In general, Robin Williams' heritage as a psychological well-being advocate keeps on rousing others to stand up, look for help, and backing those confronting psychological well-being difficulties. His obligation to destigmatize dysfunctional behavior, bringing issues to light, and elevating admittance to assets lastingly affects the discussion encompassing emotional well-being and has assisted endless people with feeling seen, heard, and upheld in their own excursions towards mending.

Personal Battles With Mental

Health issue

Robin Williams' effect on mental mindfulness is a demonstration of the force of concordance.

Through his genuine to life discussions about his own fights with distress, impulse, and disquiet, as well as his portrayal of characters dealing with close to home prosperity troubles in his motion pictures and spoof plans, Williams helped with assimilating and destigmatize mental maladjustment as per individuals overall.

By straightforwardly offering his own experiences to close to home well being issues, Williams tried speculations and misinterpretations incorporating mental maladjustment. He showed that close to home prosperity fights can impact anyone, regardless of their status or accomplishment, and that searching for help means that fortitude, not weakness.

Williams' capacity to bring humor and gentility to difficult situations also played a crucial role in shifting public perceptions of emotional health.

By including spoof as a gadget to attract jams in conversations about despairing, obsession, and other mental prosperity issues, Williams helped with making a space where people felt more open to looking at and watching out for their own fights.

Furthermore, Williams' help for emotional well-being drives and associations expanded public familiarity with the meaning of approaching assets and care for psychological well-being issues. His promotion work pointed out the way that individuals with psychological instability require seriously figuring out, compassion, and backing.

As a general rule, the tradition of Robin Williams lastingly affects public impression of emotional well-being by cultivating open correspondence, encouraging compassion and perception, and moving people to put a high need on their psychological wellness.
He has contributed to the development of a society that is more compassionate and welcoming, one in which people feel empowered to seek assistance and support when confronted with mental health issues. His willingness to tell his own story and use his platform to raise awareness of mental health issues has also contributed.

Beyond his public persona and acting career, Robin Williams had an impact on mental health and mindfulness. He used his establishment to raise resources for close to home health affiliations, support research trials, and advance drives highlighting further creating permission to mental prosperity organizations for all individuals. Williams' liberal work in the mental health space helped with driving positive change and lay out an all the more consistent environment for those fighting with broken conduct.

In spite of his efforts to help, Williams' portrayal of complex and nuanced characters in films like "Kindness Hunting," "Dead Writers Society," and "The Fisher Lord" who are dealing with emotional well-being issues helped refine these encounters and shed light on the actual factors of living with psychological illness.
His exhibitions drew large crowds and sparked significant debate regarding the significance of empathy, sympathy, and comprehension for psychological well-being.

Furthermore, Williams' legacy continues to awaken individuals to zero in on their mental success and search for help when required. He exhibited that it is feasible to conquer difficulty and track down recuperating through treatment, prescription, and backing from friends and family by offering his own excursion to emotional wellness issues. His message of optimism and perseverance can serve as a beacon for those struggling with their own mental health issues.

Advocacy For Mental Health Awareness And Support

Throughout his life, Robin Williams was an ardent proponent of mental health support and awareness. He involved his foundation as a darling entertainer and humorist to talk straightforwardly about his own battles with misery, habit, and tension, breaking down the shame encompassing dysfunctional behavior and empowering others to look for help.

Williams' backing for psychological wellness issues was profoundly private, as he frequently imparted his own encounters to wretchedness and fixation in meetings and public appearances. By sharing his story, he assisted with adapting the experience of living with dysfunctional behavior and demonstrated the way that even somebody as fruitful and darling as himself could battle with these issues.

As well as talking straightforwardly about his own psychological wellness challenges, Williams likewise utilized his acclaim to bring issues to light and assets for emotional wellness associations and drives. He took part in foundation occasions, pledge drives, and public missions pointed toward destigmatizing dysfunctional behavior, advancing emotional well-being schooling, and offering help for people out of luck.

Robin Williams' involvement with the Christopher & Dana Reeve Foundation, which provides assistance to people living with paralysis and spinal cord injuries, is one of the most well-known ways in which he worked to raise awareness of mental health issues. Williams was a dear companion of Christopher Reeve and devoted his time and assets to bringing issues to light about the effect of these circumstances on psychological wellness and prosperity.

Besides, Williams upheld associations like the St. Jude Children's Research Hospital, which gives care and treatment to kids confronting difficult ailments, including emotional wellness conditions. His humanitarian endeavors stretched out past his own battles to include a more extensive obligation to supporting people of any age who were wrestling with emotional well-being difficulties.

Generally, Robin Williams' promotion for psychological wellness mindfulness and backing was a demonstration of his sympathy, compassion, and obligation to helping other people. By sharing his own story, supporting worthy missions, and utilizing his foundation to bring issues to light, Williams passed on an enduring heritage that keeps on rousing discussions about psychological wellness and advancing a more empathetic and grasping society for those confronting comparative difficulties.

Beyond his public persona as a beloved entertainer, Robin Williams had an impact on mental health advocacy. He likewise utilized his ability and imagination to acquire consideration regarding psychological well-being issues in his work, frequently consolidating subjects of psychological wellness, strength, and the significance of looking for help in his exhibitions.

In his jobs in movies, for example, "Good Will Hunting," "Dead Poets Society," and "Good Morning, Vietnam," Williams depicted characters who wrestled with unseen conflicts, injury, and personal difficulties. Through these nuanced depictions, he brought a feeling of vagueness and compassion to the screen, revealing insight into the intricacies of emotional wellness and the force of human association in beating difficulty.

Williams' comedic virtuoso was likewise a wellspring of solace and motivation for some people battling with psychological well-being issues. His fast mind, humor, and capacity to find delicacy in dim minutes reverberated with crowds all over the planet, offering a feeling of trust and fellowship to the people who felt segregated or got in their own battles wrong.

Notwithstanding his on-screen work, Williams involved his stand-up parody schedules as a stage to address troublesome points like sorrow, dependence, and tension. Through his crude and fair narrating, he associated with crowds on a profoundly private level, welcoming them to snicker, cry, and consider their own encounters with psychological well-being.

Past his expert undertakings, Williams additionally upheld various emotional well-being associations and drives through his magnanimity and promotion work. He volunteered his time, resources, and skills to promote accessibility to mental health care, reduce mental illness stigma, and increase public awareness of mental health issues.

The legacy of Robin Williams serves as a beacon of hope and understanding in a world where people struggling with mental health issues frequently experience silence or shame. His boldness in sharing his own story, his devotion to supporting others out of luck, and his steady obligation to destigmatizing psychological maladjustment keep on motivating people and networks to focus on emotional wellness, mindfulness, sympathy, and backing for all.

Impact On Public Perfection Of Mental Health

Williams impact on mental health awareness
is a testament to the power of honesty

Williams' dependence issues were interlaced with his emotional wellness challenges, as he looked for alleviation from the extraordinary sensations of misery, uneasiness, and depression that tormented him.

Williams sought professional assistance for his addiction and mental health issues throughout his life, enrolling in rehab programs and attending therapy sessions to address his underlying issues. He was determined to have bipolar turmoil, a condition portrayed by outrageous emotional episodes, which further muddled his psychological wellness venture. Williams' encounters with psychological maladjustment were intricate and diverse, incorporating times of extraordinary inventiveness and efficiency as well as episodes of profound despondency and dimness.

Notwithstanding his battles, Williams stayed focused on bringing issues to light about emotional wellness and upholding for others confronting comparable difficulties. He talked truly about his own fights with gloom and dependence in meetings and public appearances, utilizing his foundation to destigmatize psychological maladjustment and urge others to look for help.

Many people were inspired to open up about their own struggles and seek support for their mental health issues by Williams' vulnerability and honesty in sharing his story.

At last, Williams' passing was a sad indication of the overwhelming effect of untreated emotional wellness conditions and the significance of focusing on one's prosperity. His inheritance fills in as a strong sign of the requirement for sympathy, understanding, and compassion towards those wrestling with psychological wellness issues, as well as the basic significance of admittance to quality psychological wellness care and assets.

The personal struggles that Robin Williams had with his mental health have had a long-lasting impact on the discussion about mental illness, bringing to light the complexity of these conditions and the difficulties they face.

Robin Williams' own fights with psychological well-being issues were a powerful indication of the way that dysfunctional behavior doesn't segregate, influencing people from varying backgrounds, no matter what their popularity or achievement. Williams' battles shed light on the unavoidable idea of psychological well-being difficulties and the significance of breaking down the disgrace encompassing these issues.

In spite of his gigantic ability and prominence, Williams' internal conflict and close to home agony were profoundly felt, featuring the way that emotional well-being conditions can affect anybody, no matter what their outer conditions. His readiness to talk transparently about his battles assisted with refining the experience of living with dysfunctional behavior and urged others to look for help and backing when required.

Williams' passing was a heartbreaking misfortune that highlighted the overwhelming outcomes of untreated psychological well-being conditions and the critical requirement for expanded mindfulness, schooling, and assets to help those wrestling with dysfunctional behavior.
Williams' heritage keeps on rousing discussions about psychological wellness, destigmatize conversations encompassing these issues, and advance sympathy and understanding towards people confronting comparative difficulties.

In thinking about Robin Williams' own fights with emotional wellness, we are helped to remember the significance of sympathy, compassion, and backing for those exploring their own psychological wellness ventures.

The story of Williams is a powerful reminder that mental health issues can affect anyone and that seeking help is a sign of strength rather than weakness. By considering his memory and proceeding to advocate for psychological well-being, mindfulness and assets, we can pursue making a more humane and steady society for all people confronting emotional well-being difficulties.

Chapter 6

Conclusion

Final Years And Legacy

In the last long periods of his life, Robin Williams confronted various individual and wellbeing challenges that eventually added to his shocking passing by self destruction in 2014. Regardless of his colossal ability and outcome in media outlets, Williams battled with misery, nervousness, and dependence all through his life. His fights with substance misuse and psychological well-being issues were indisputable, and he was open about his battles with enslavement and his endeavors to keep up with his restraint.

In the years paving the way to his demise, Williams encountered a decrease in his emotional wellness and confronted monetary troubles because of an exorbitant separation and progressing fights in court.

He likewise got a finding of Parkinson's sickness, an ever-evolving neurological confusion that can fundamentally affect mental and actual prosperity. These difficulties negatively affected Williams' emotional wellness and added to sensations of sadness and gloom.

Robin Williams' heritage as a dearest entertainer, entertainer, and philanthropic keeps on persevering.

Notwithstanding his amusement vocation, Williams was known for his generosity and promotion work on the side of different causes, including emotional well-being, mindfulness, vagrancy, and youngsters' foundations. He utilized his foundation to raise assets for associations like St. Jude Children's Research Hospital,Lighthearted element, and the Christopher and Dana Reeve Establishment, exhibiting his obligation to having a beneficial outcome on the world.

Fans, family, and friends of Robin Williams continue to honor his life and work, preserving his legacy. His commitments to media outlets and his endeavors to bring issues to light about psychological wellness have made a permanent imprint on society. Williams' readiness to impart his own battles to dysfunctional behavior assisted with diminishing shame and rousing others to look for help and backing when required.

At last, Robin Williams' last years were set apart by both individual difficulties and persevering through achievements. While his demise was a significant misfortune for the world, his heritage as a gifted entertainer, sympathetic, helpful, and psychological well-being advocate proceeds to rouse and resonate with individuals, all things considered.

Tributes And Commemorations

After Robin Williams' terrible passing in 2014, there was an overflow of accolades and remembrances to respect his life, heritage, and commitments to media outlets. The following are some of the most notable memorials and tributes:

1. Public Remembrances:
Fans all over the planet coordinated public dedications and get-togethers to honor Robin Williams. These occasions frequently highlighted screenings of his most cherished films, live exhibitions of his stand-up schedules, and ardent talks praising his life and work.

2.Social Media Entertainment Accolades:
Virtual entertainment stages were overwhelmed with accolades from VIPs, fans, and associates sharing recollections, photographs, and messages of appreciation for Williams' effect on their lives. The hashtag #RIPRobinWilliams moved around the world as individuals shared their #1 minute and statements from his vocation.

3. Award Show Tributes:
A few honor shows, including the Oscars, Brilliant Globes, and Emmys, honored Robin Williams during their functions. Clasps of his notable exhibitions were shown, and partners and

companions talked about his ability, generosity, and effect on media outlets.

4. Beneficent Commitments:
Many of Robin Williams's fans and organizations gave to the St. Jude Children's Research Hospital, the Christopher & Dana Reeve Foundation, and the United States of America in memory of his philanthropic efforts during his lifetime.

5. Devoted Exhibitions:
Comics and entertainers honored Robin Williams by integrating components of his humor, style, and characters into their own exhibitions. A few humorists even committed whole sets to observing Williams' comedic virtuoso and effect on the universe of comedy.

6. Tribute. Movies:
Soon after his passing, a few narratives and biopics were delivered that investigated Robin Williams' life, vocation, battles with psychological well-being, and getting through heritage. These movies offered fans a more profound comprehension of the man behind the chuckling and praised his enduring effect on media outlets.

7. Legacy Undertakings:
To respect Robin Williams' memory, different tasks and drives were sent off in his name, including grants for trying entertainers, emotional well being mindfulness missions, and film celebrations

exhibiting his work. These endeavors aimed to carry on his legacy of wit, compassion, and creativity.

8. Tributes in Art:
Craftsmen and artists made shocking representations, works of art, and advanced craftsmanship to pay tribute to Robin Williams, displaying his notorious characters and vital exhibitions. To honor his influence on popular culture, these artistic tributes were displayed in galleries and shared on social media.

9. Musical References:
Artists and groups honored Robin Williams through unique exhibitions, cover tunes, and unique arrangements propelled by his life and work. A few specialists even committed whole shows to praising his humor, mind, and humankind through music.

10. Roasts with Comedy:
Satire clubs and scenes facilitated extraordinary meal evenings committed to respecting Robin Williams, where joke artists affectionately made fun of his comedic style, improvisational abilities, and remarkable characters. These occasions gave a carefree method for praising his heritage and carrying giggling to crowds.

11. Education initiatives:
Schools, colleges, and instructive foundations created educational plan units and studios zeroed

in on concentrating on Robin Williams' commitments to parody, acting, and narrating. Understudies had the chance to investigate his assorted group of work and dissect the effect of his exhibitions on mainstream society.

12. Virtual Commemorations:
Online stages and sites made virtual commemorations and intelligent encounters where fans could share their number one recollections of Robin Williams, leave messages of recognition, and partake in virtual occasions committed to praising his life and vocation. These computerized recognitions permitted fans from around the world to meet up in respecting his heritage.

13.Celebrity charity events;
In honor of Robin Williams, prominent figures in the entertainment industry held charity events, auctions, and fundraisers, with the proceeds going to comedy foundations, mental health organizations, and humanitarian causes he supported during his lifetime. His determination to assist the less fortunate was made clear by these occurrences.

14. Legacy Products:
Organizations and brands delivered restricted release stock, for example, shirts, banners, and collectibles highlighting notable statements, pictures, and characters related to Robin Williams. The returns from the deals of these things were

frequently given to altruistic associations in his honor.

15. Fan Tributes:
Fans made fan-made recordings, montages, and fan fiction stories committed to observing Robin Williams' vocation and effect on their lives. These sincere tributes showed how much his work meant to his fans and how he influenced future generations of viewers.

The different scope of recognitions and celebrations following Robin Williams' passing mirror the significant impact he had on media outlets and the persevering through affection and reverence fans keep on holding for him. His inheritance lives on through the endless manners by which he has been praised and recollected by individuals from varying backgrounds.

In general, the recognitions and celebrations following Robin Williams' passing filled in as a demonstration of his persevering through effect on media outlets and the hearts of millions of fans around the world. His inheritance keeps on being praised through his immortal exhibitions, beneficent undertakings, and the permanent imprint he left on the universe of satire and acting.

Lasting impact On The

Entertainment industry

Robin Williams' enduring effect on media outlets is certain and extensive. Williams' unmatched talent, versatility, and ability to improvise pushed the boundaries of comedy and acting throughout his career. His remarkable mix of humor, mind, and genuine exhibitions enamored crowds of any age and foundations, procuring him a committed following and basic praise.

Williams' famous jobs in movies, for example, "Dead Poets Society," "Good Will Hunting," and "Good Morning, Vietnam" displayed his outstanding reach as an entertainer and procured him various honors, including a Foundation Grant for Best Supporting Entertainer for his job in "Good Will Hunting." His capacity to flawlessly progress among comedic and sensational jobs exhibited his flexibility and profundity as an entertainer, hardening his status as one of the most regarded and cherished entertainers of his age.

Notwithstanding his film work, Williams had a massive effect on TV with his job as Mork in the hit sitcom "Mork and Mindy," which shot him to fame in the last part of the 1970s. His irresistible enthusiasm, quick fire humor, and charming appeal charmed him to crowds all over the planet and assisted with laying him out as a comedic force to be reckoned with in Hollywood.

Past his on-screen exhibitions, Williams' impact stretched out to the universe of stand-up satire, where he was known for his charging stage presence, extremely sharp mind, and uncanny capacity to make do on the spot. His stand-up specials, including "Robin Williams:Live in the Met" and

"Robin Williams: Live on Broadway," displayed his comedic genius and solidified his standing as one of the best humorists ever.

Besides, Williams' effect on media outlets was not restricted to his work before the camera. He was likewise a capable voice entertainer, loaning his particular voice to cherished vivified characters like Genie in Disney's "Aladdin" and Ramon in "Blissful Feet." His voice work rejuvenated these characters with humor, warmth, and character, further exhibiting his flexibility and inventiveness as an entertainer.

Generally, Robin Williams' enduring effect on media outlets can be felt in the getting through fame of his movies, network shows, and stand-up schedules, as well as in the incalculable lives he contacted with his ability, liberality, and sympathy. His heritage as a comedic virtuoso, flexible entertainer, and dearest performer proceeds to move and engage crowds all over the planet, guaranteeing that his memory will live on for a long time into the future.

Printed in Great Britain
by Amazon

40741282R00059